AMERICAN PRISO
AT DARTMOOR
(1813-1

By Trevor James

ORCHARD PUBLICATIONS
2 Orchard Close, Chudleigh, Devon TQ13 0LR
Telephone: (01626) 852714

ISBN 9781898964803

Printed by
Hedgerow Print, Crediton, Devon EX17 1ES

i

Contents

Introduction   1

Foreword   2

Dartmoor Prison of War   5

A Prisoner's Life at Dartmoor   10

An American Depot   14

The Final Episode   18

Last Days   23

Significant dates   28

INTRODUCTION

Dartmoor, in the county of Devon, is a plateau of approximately 360 square miles and a maximum height of 2,039 feet above sea level. It embraces large areas of grassland, rocky hills (known as tors), river valleys and numerous farms and villages. The remains of ancient tin workings, granite quarries, prehistoric hut circles and stone rows are abundant, but the most astonishing sight to be seen are the bleak group of buildings within the walls of Dartmoor Prison.

Dartmoor Depot as it was first called was built between 1806 and 1809 at the instigation of local landowner Sir Thomas Tyrwhitt who founded the little settlement at Princetown. It had been decided that an additional War Depot should be built in Devon to ease the congestion among the French prisoners of war held on the prison ships at Plymouth. Sir Thomas held several important posts and was a close friend of the Prince of Wales (the heir to the throne) who owned the land where the proposed depot was to be. Both men saw an opportunity to profit from

Sir Thomas Tyrwhitt. Photo courtesy of Paul Rendell and reproduced by permission of the Governing Body, Christchurch, Oxford.)

the venture: a leasehold rent would be payable to the Prince (Prince Charles is the present landlord) and Sir Thomas would profit from his quarries from which much of the building stone would be taken. The first French prisoners entered the depot in May 1809 and were joined by Americans in April 1813. In 1814 after the war with France was over Dartmoor became the place of confinement for all American prisoners in Britain, more than 5,500 of them.

The area has a long established reputation for bad weather. The cold and the wet and the frequent fogs added to the misery of the French and Americans who first lived here and of the convicts of a later era. Today Dartmoor is a National Park and the prison is a training establishment for low grade prisoners. Princetown is fast becoming the main attraction for visitors to Dartmoor for the spectacular scenery that surrounds it but more especially because of a fascination for the famous prison and its history.

FOREWORD

The year 1812 was a critical one for Britain. The country had been at war with France since 1803 with no sign of victory despite the spectacular defeat of the combined French and Spanish fleets at Trafalgar in 1805 which at least ensured mastery of the seas and prevented Napoleon's planned invasion of England. Nevertheless almost all of Europe was now under French control, from Spain to the Baltic and from France itself to Italy and the borders of Russia. The British army under the command of the Duke of Wellington was regrouping in Portugal even though they'd won a series of battles against the French in Spain. The 'Iron Duke' could not continue the offensive until replacements arrived for those killed and wounded; there was also a shortage of supplies and heavy guns (the Spanish had rebelled against French rule and the objective of the 'Peninsula War', as it came to be called, was to free that country and invade France from the south). In England there was rioting over food shortages after bad harvests. To cap it all King George III was suffering from another bout of mental illness and the Prince of Wales (the future King George IV) ruled in his place as Prince Regent. Now he and his government stood practically alone in defiance of the French Empire.

It might be thought things could not get much worse but a severe setback occurred on 18th June 1812 when the United States declared war after a series of disputes and unresolved grievances with Britain. The British now faced a conflict on two fronts – the French on the continent of Europe and another in America where the war spread to parts of Canada (where President Madison's administration claimed certain territorial rights) and on the Great Lakes. Sea battles occurred worldwide from British home waters and the Atlantic to the Pacific Ocean.

A problem of yet another kind reached a peak that year. Thanks to the successful Royal Navy blockade of European ports and in the aftermath of Trafalgar, vast numbers of French prisoners of war were taken, mostly sailors, but there was an acute shortage of accommodation for them. All the war prisons were full and as a temporary measure more than forty redundant warships were converted to prison ships – the 'Hulks' as they were called. With the continuous influx of prisoners they became a feature of prisoner of war confinement for the duration of the wars. Twelve of these prison ships were at anchor in Plymouth. Prisoners were kept below decks except for half an hour during the day when they were allowed out in relays for a some fresh air. At night the wooden ports on the ships' sides and entrances to below decks were fastened shut. Typhus, chest infections and other diseases were rampant because of the foetid atmosphere, lack of exercise and a poor diet.

The Dartmoor Prison of War Depot in Princetown opened in 1809 having been built specifically to help alleviate the dreadful overcrowding that prevailed on the hulks together with the accompanying rise in the death rate of prisoners. By 1812, in the wake of Wellington's first Spanish campaign previously mentioned, the Depot was filled to capacity and had found it necessary to construct two extra prison blocks which in turn soon filled with inmates.

Britain had her back to the wall in the fight against Napoleon who was at the zenith of his career and very much 'Master of Europe'. With the finest units of the British army fighting to retain a foothold in Spain and Portugal another conflict, this time with America, was a huge burden on resources. Many thousands of French prisoners were crammed into the stinking hulks where they died in their hundreds. Large numbers of them were transferred to Dartmoor Depot where hundreds more died. The teeming mass of humanity, the diseases, suicides, and moral despair of some prisoners made a veritable hell hole of both locations.

The dreaded hulks. (From a painting by Paul Deacon)

Into these appalling conditions were thrust American prisoners of war. At Plymouth they were confined on board the *Hector*, *Ceres* and *El Ferme*. Other Americans were sent to the hulks at Gosport (near Portsmouth) and Chatham as well as to the Depots at Stapleton, near Bristol, Normans Cross near Peterborough and a few (mainly sick men) to Mill Prison in Plymouth. They were all at a later date destined to go to Dartmoor.

Note: *American officers were sent to Ashburton to live 'On Parole', a concession already granted to hundreds of French officers in other towns around Dartmoor. This meant they either rented accommodation or lodged with local families, living as free men provided they observed the conditions of parole signed and sworn to by them. They undertook not to try and escape; to obey the laws of England; not to communicate with the enemy; to observe the curfew times as instructed by the local Agent appointed to supervise them; and to attend roll calls as required.*

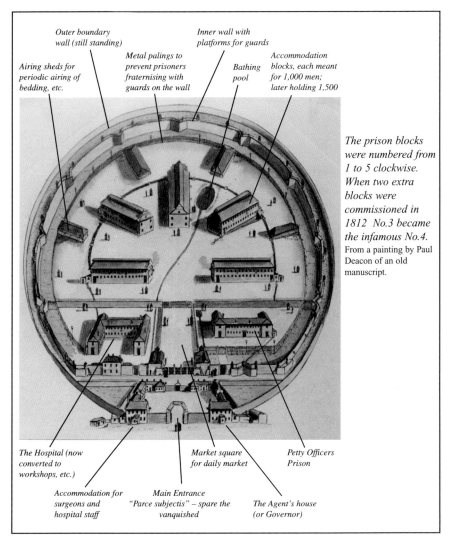

Outer boundary wall (still standing)

Inner wall with platforms for guards

Airing sheds for periodic airing of bedding, etc.

Metal palings to prevent prisoners fraternising with guards on the wall

Bathing pool

Accommodation blocks, each meant for 1,000 men; later holding 1,500

The prison blocks were numbered from 1 to 5 clockwise. When two extra blocks were commissioned in 1812 No.3 became the infamous No.4. From a painting by Paul Deacon of an old manuscript.

The Hospital (now converted to workshops, etc.)

Market square for daily market

Petty Officers Prison

Accommodation for surgeons and hospital staff

Main Entrance "Parce subjectis" – spare the vanquished

The Agent's house (or Governor)

DARTMOOR PRISON OF WAR

The previous page shows what the Depot looked like in 1810. There were two boundary walls, an inner one no longer standing, and an outer wall about one mile in circumference. This is the surrounding wall you see today. The space between them was known as the Military Walk – a sort of no-mans-land to help prevent escapes. Note the triangular platforms on the inner wall where sentries were posted to observe and guard the prison. The bathing pool was a great comfort to the men with running water conducted by gravity (the ground slopes from the front to the rear of the prison) from a reservoir situated opposite the main entrance. This in turn was fed by a shallow canal or 'leat' which took water from the River Walkham four miles away. Drinking water came from the same source.

The prison blocks were approximately 140 feet long and 40 feet wide. They were each designed to accommodate 1,000 men, 500 on each of the first two floors, which were constructed of concrete, and a third level with wooden flooring intended for recreation when the weather was bad. All three floors were later pressed into service when more and more captives arrived and as mentioned already, in 1811 two extra prison blocks were built to ease the overcrowding. The living quarters were sparse indeed, consisting of open dormitories each with long rows of metal posts from which to sling the hammocks the prisoners were issued with. As the place filled to capacity these were slung one above the other as many as five high. There was no furniture of any kind, no heating arrangements and the windows were simply 2 feet square unglazed apertures with wooden shutters through which the freezing draught must have howled during the winter months. As it happened the crush of closely packed bodies kept them reasonably warm and they must have stuffed clothing and rags into the gaps in the shutters to improve matters. The resulting stale air did not improve their health though and this was later proved to have been the cause of the several illnesses suffered by the inmates, most of whom were sailors. They were fit and healthy when captured but deteriorated without the physical work they were used to and the conditions they were compelled to live under.

Their rations too were a contributory factor and they were always hungry. The supplies were contracted out and although representatives chosen by the men themselves inspected what was delivered there was much scope for deception and more than one contractor had his contract cancelled as well as being fined or even imprisoned.

French and American Prisoners of War – Table of Daily Ration

Days	Bread	Beef	Codfish	Herrings	Potatoes	Greens	Scotch Barley	Onions	Salt
	lb.	lb.	lb.	lb.	lb.	lb.	oz.	oz.	oz
Sunday	1.5	0.5	~	~	~	0.5	1.0	qtr	third
Monday	1.5	0.5	~	~	~	0.5	1.0	qtr	third
Tuesday	1.5	0.5	~	~	~	0.5	1.0	qtr	third
Wednesday	1.5	~	~	1.0	1.0	~	~	~	~
Thursday	1.5	0.5	~	~	~	0.5	1.0	qtr	third
Friday	1.5	~	1.0	~	1.0	~	~	~	~
Saturday	1.5	0.5	~	~	~	0.5	1.0	qtr	third
TOTAL	10.5	2.5	1.0	1.0	2.0	2.5	5.0	$1^{1}/_{4}$	$1^{2}/_{3}$

Bread	To be made of Wheaten Meal.
Beef	To be good and wholesome fresh Beef, not Bull Beef, and delivered in clean Quarters, a Fore and Hind Quarter alternately.
Cod-Fish	To be the produce of the Fishery at Newfoundland, or the Coast of Labrador; and to be delivered in whole Fish.
Herrings	To be good and sound; and Red and White Herrings to be issued alternately

Potatoes, Greens, Turnips, and Onions

To be good in their respective kinds. The Greens to be stripped of outside leaves, and fit for the Copper.

At first sight the rations seem reasonable except for quantity. Agreements had been made with the enemy to provide a basic standard of subsistence and this was generally adhered to. The problem arose with the quality of the provisions and how they were prepared. Every man's ration went to the cookhouse where the ingredients were boiled in communal cauldrons and issued for messes of six men. One American prisoner (Charles Andrews) describes collecting the allowance in wooden buckets around which the six prisoners would sit on the floor and eat with wooden spoons.

The market square was a focal point for everyone when a market was held there every day except Sundays from 9 a.m. until 12 noon. Local farmers and traders from Tavistock and as far away as Plymouth attended to sell or barter their wares which included poultry, coffee, tobacco, vegetables, items of clothing

The Market Square and Prisoners of War (Painting by a Dartmoor Prison inmate). Note the water supply conduits.

– in fact every small comfort a prisoner might need. Prisoners always had the free use of the open spaces around the prison blocks but not the market square except during trading times when the lower gates would be opened to allow access.

To the right of the square was the 'Petty Officers Prison'. This was a separate place of imprisonment for officers who either broke their terms of parole or declined to accept parole. Here the French officers lived a life of relative luxury, employing ships' boys from among the common inmates to wait upon them, clean and do their laundry etc. Many of them received sums of money forwarded to them from their families at home which enabled them to purchase the best of food from the daily market.

To the left of the market square was the hospital manned by a Royal Navy Surgeon, a Matron and three Attendants. They were assisted by a number of ancillary nurses recruited from prisoners in good health. They were paid sixpence a day and enjoyed the improved hospital diet to help keep them healthy. A valued 'perk' was the clothing of men who died which could be sold to other inmates if not needed for themselves. The dead were examined to ascertain the cause of death before being taken to the 'Dead House' which was simply a stone hut outside the prison walls. When it was full the bodies were interred in rough coffins on the open moor without ceremony or religious rites of any kind. Between 1809 and 1816 more than 1450 Frenchmen died, 500 of them from an outbreak of measles during the first winter they were there. The Americans lost 271 all told, most of them from an epidemic of what came to be called the 'African Pox', a particularly virulent form of smallpox.

To the right of the main entrance was the home of the Agent or Governor.

Responsibility for all prisoners of war in Britain lay with the Transport Office, a subsidiary of the Admiralty, and the term 'Agent' refers to the representative of that Office who took charge of prisoners either in the prisons, the hulks or on parole. A strict set of rules applied for the issue of clothing and bedding, the correct amount of rations, and methods of controlling unruly men. Corporal punishment (flogging etc.) was forbidden by mutual agreement with the foe. Instead use was made of a miniature prison approximately 20 feet square made of stone but without windows or heating or bedding and secured by a thick door with metal plates. It was called the Cachot but was invariably referred to as 'The Black Hole' which it truly was. Men who misbehaved were put into this infamous hovel to lie on a stone floor in the dark and on two thirds rations for a maximum of ten days at the discretion of the Agent. Some poor wretches died of the cold in the winter months. Serious offences were dealt with by the courts.

Excerpts from the regulations for Prisoners of war in the Depots and on the Hulks appertaining to Punishment in the 'Black Hole'.

The prisoners are forbidden to strike, menace or insult, any Officer, Turnkey, or other person employed in the prisons or prison Ships, under pain of losing their Turn of Exchange*, of being closely confined in the Black Hole, and forfeiting one third of their rations...

* *There were periodic exchanges of prisoners from both sides on the basis of man for man according to rank.*

...are forbidden to fight, quarrel or excite any Tumult or Disorder in the Prisons or prison Ships, or in the places where they shall be allowed to take the Air, under pain of being confined in the Black Hole and forfeiting one third of their ration for a time proportional to the offence.

Any prisoner who shall be taken *attempting* to escape shall be put in the Black Hole for ten days, and shall lose his Turn of Exchange (author's italics).

...any prisoner who shall be retaken *after having escaped* from the Prison or prison Ships, and shall by this means have occasioned Expense, shall not only lose his Turn of Exchange, and be put in the Black Hole, but shall, *with the whole of the Prisoners kept on the same deck or room from which he has escaped*, be reduced to one third of their Ration until, by such reduction, the Expenses shall be made good, and *even if he should not be retaken*, the whole of the Prisoners in the same manner to reimburse the Expenses of attending such escape (author's italics)

A Market is allowed...but the Prisoners are forbidden to buy or introduce into the prison, Liquor, Knives or Weapons of any kind under pain of being confined in the Black Hole for Ten Days for such offence.

The prisoners are allowed during market hours to sell articles of their own manufacture, except Mittens, Woollen Gloves, Straw Hats, or Bonnets, Shoes, Plaited Straw, Obscene Pictures, or Images, and articles formed of the Prison Stores which are strictly forbidden, and any Prisoner selling or making any of these Articles...shall be confined in the Black Hole, and reduced to two thirds of his Ration for three days...and such Articles shall be destroyed.

Any prisoner who shall have bought, sold, or disposed of his Ration by gambling or otherwise, or shall have sold or made away with any article of clothing, even though such Articles belong to him, shall be confined in the Black Hole, and shall only receive two thirds of his Ration during such time as the Agent may direct, and lose his Turn of Exchange.

These were some of the guidelines upon which the Agents acted to enforce discipline and order in the Establishments under their charge.

Dartmoor Prison entrance arch. (Drawing by Paul Deacon) The famous stone archway under which thousands of unhappy men marched into captivity all those years ago. The Latin words 'PARCERE SUBJECTIS' (Spare the Vanquished) are inscribed overhead.

The early 19th century was an age of exaggerated good manners and chivalry among the upper classes. It was also an age of extreme brutality and enough has been said already to illustrate the latter at Dartmoor Depot.

A PRISONER'S LIFE AT DARTMOOR

The first batch of 250 American prisoners were disembarked from the hulk *Hector* on 3rd April 1813 and marched to Dartmoor under heavy escort. The moor was covered with a layer of snow and we can imagine their apprehension as they caught sight of the grim grey walls of the stone fortress which was to be their home.

All the depots and some of the hulks were guarded by units of Militia drawn from all over Britain, supported by regular soldiers. They were replaced at intervals, usually every three months, to prevent them becoming friendly with the prisoners which could lead to some of them assisting a prisoner to escape in return for a bribe. The Militiamen were poorly paid and recruited mainly from the lower classes, many of whom would use any means to obtain money for drink. Should one of them be caught aiding an inmate the least he could expect was a flogging and some were shot. By the time the Americans began arriving the number of guards had increased from around 500 in 1809 to more than 1200 due mainly to the increase in the prison population and because the Yankees had an unruly reputation (it is a fact they were defiant and troublesome throughout their stay). The troops were quartered in a barracks adjacent to the Depot. Little remains of the barracks today and the site has been developed for housing. The officers lived and messed in what is now the High Moorland Visitors Centre in Princetown.

This old photo of the Duchy Hotel, now the High Moorland Visitor Centre in Princetown, illustrates how it must have looked when it was the Militia Officer's Mess. (Photo courtesy of Brian Dingle).

On arrival all prisoners were interviewed by the clerks who recorded their details in what was known as the General Entry Book. This was standard procedure in all the depots, prison ships, and parole locations. Most of these record books survive in the Public Record Office at Kew (Surrey), enabling us to get a very accurate description of each one of the 100,000 and more French and American prisoners imprisoned in Britain during the two wars. The entries for every man recorded his name, age, rank, name of ship or military unit, where captured (latitude and longitude for sailors) and a description of his physical appearance. This included height, build, colour of hair and eyes, complexion, facial features and distinguishing marks or tattoos. Not only was this information invaluable in case of escape but we today gain a priceless 'word picture' of these men, many of whom have descendants who would wish to know their background and what they looked like. In addition, the date of arrival was written down and in due course the manner of departure i.e.

E = Exchanged. A possibility already noted and what every man hoped for.
R = Run (escaped).There were several successful escapes.
D = Discharged. Indicates transfer to another depot or back to the hulks. When the wars ended all prisoners were discharged and repatriated in which case the port of departure and destination was also noted.
DD = Discharged dead.

The men were issued with hammocks and bedding (straw filled mattresses) and some clothing. In the early days they were given a woollen hat, jacket, trousers, two shirts, two pairs of stockings and canvas shoes with wooden soles. By 1812 the cost of the wars forced the Agents to economise and what was issued depended on the condition of the clothes they wore on arrival. Everything they got was written down on a 'ticket'. The ticket had to be produced before any worn out item could be replaced and on departure, transfer or release, everything listed had to be returned (it is on record that a Frenchman was actually at the prison gate ready to leave for home when he was restrained because he could not produce his bedding. He cut his own throat in a fit of despair). The dormitories described previously were viewed with disdain by the newcomers who referred to them as 'horse stables'. They also refused to eat the Scotch Barley included in their rations which they called 'burgoo' and claimed to feed it only to animals at home.

At the time of the Americans' arrival the prison was desperately crowded and there was resentment among the Frenchmen, some of whom had been captives there for three years. Many of them were employed as barbers, sweepers, and cooks; others worked on various projects including repairing roads and the building of Princetown Church. As forced labour was forbidden they were paid up to sixpence per day and in most cases the money they earned soon found its way to the gambling tables and card games which were the sole recreations available to them. Other prisoners manufactured model ships and a variety of knick-knacks for sale or barter at market. Some beautiful examples can be seen today in Plymouth Museum and Art Gallery.

Model ship made from meat bones by a Dartmoor prisoner of war. (Photo courtesy of Plymouth Museum and Art Gallery)

There was a downside however. A number of them without jobs or skills degenerated in the wake of despair or sheer idleness to the extent they sold or gambled away everything they had – bedding, clothes, even their rations. They ended up filthy vice- ridden wretches of the lowest order. Naked and starving they hunted for scraps in the gutters and were reviled by their fellow countrymen who at last banished them to the top level of No. 4 block where they adopted the title 'Romans'. The yard adjacent to this block was enclosed by a wall to prevent the occupants from mixing with the other prisoners. It was to this very prison block the American prisoners were consigned to – a horrible fate made worse by them being forbidden the freedom of the other yards and the market on the orders of the Agent Captain Isaac Cotgrave, Royal Navy. Within a short time the Yankees were in a sorry state and at the mercy of the French who were quick to take advantage of them. Desperate men bartered their clothes and their food for a chew of tobacco or a little coffee. Relations with the 'Romans' were less then cordial as you might expect and culminated in a brawl one morning when the French armed themselves with home made knives and cudgels and set about the unarmed Americans. Around twenty men on both sides needed hospital treatment. The authorities then built a dividing wall in the yard to keep the two sides apart and in October 1813 the Romans were ejected and sent back to the Plymouth hulks for the rest of their captivity.

There was more misery to be endured before matters improved. In the autumn of that year there was an outbreak of smallpox. Regardless of this Captain Cotgrave insisted upon a daily roll call with no regard to the weather or the pitiful condition of the Americans, many of whom were now clothed in rags and some barefooted (worn out clothing was supposed to be replaced periodically but in many instances this was not done). Many a man collapsed in the freezing cold only to be left where they lay until the roll call was completed.

The turning point for the Yankees came on 22nd. December 1813 when Captain Cotgrave resigned and his place taken by Captain Thomas Shortland, Royal Navy. One of his first acts was to permit them to attend the market. The daily roll calls ceased and later on they were allowed to stroll around all the yards at will. Every man was then issued with fresh clothing- jacket, waistcoat, pantaloons, a woollen cap and canvas shoes with wooden soles just before the terrible winter of 1813/14 when buckets of water froze solid in a matter of hours and snow drifts reached the top of the boundary walls. It was the worst winter in living memory.

The Americans now emulated the French in constructing various trinkets and models to barter with. In February 1814 their government authorised a payment to every man of one and a half pence per day with which to purchase tobacco and soap. Soon they were able to set up market stalls of their own selling clothes, shoes, and little luxuries concocted from ingredients bought at the regular market. The following month their allowance was increased to a total of six shillings and eight pence* per man payable every 32 days. The extra payments were intended for the purchase of coffee and sugar from the market traders but in fact it was almost invariably spent at the gambling sessions which had now become a feature of everyday life.

This represented a third of one pound sterling at that time.

A turning point had also been reached on the Continent. Napoleon had invaded Russia in 1812 with disastrous results. Out of the 500,000 men in his 'Grand Army' a mere 20,000 survived the winter retreat from Moscow. The Duke of Wellington and his army had won spectacular victories in Spain, crossed the Pyrenees and were advancing northwards across France. Russian and Austrian armies were closing in from the east supported by Prussian units and by 11th. April they were at the gates of Paris. The game was up for the Emperor and he abdicated that very day. The French war was over.

At Dartmoor the French prisoners began departing for home, a move that was accelerated on instructions from the Transport Office to Captain Shortland to clear the place of French prisoners *'with as little delay as possible'*. The Depot had been selected for the confinement of all American prisoners of war in Britain.

AN AMERICAN DEPOT

By the end of June 1814 all the French had gone home, Napoleon had agreed to live in exile on the Mediterranean island of Elba, and the Americans had Dartmoor Depot to themselves. That same month Captain Shortland called for volunteers to do the jobs vacated by the departing Frenchmen. Labourers were needed to maintain the roads, carpenters and nurses, sweepers, cooks, barbers etc. Princetown Church was still under construction at this time and it fell to the Americans to finish the job which they did in fine style. There was no shortage of applicants to earn a little extra money. Sadly most of their earnings were spent gambling; accounts by prisoners who were there describe the bedlam that prevailed night after night with disputes and fights until the early hours. In an effort to stop it Shortland threatened to close the daily market but to no avail. There was little else for the men to occupy themselves.

Princetown Parish Church of St. Michael and All Angels. Built by French and American prisoners of war.

Soon Yankee prisoners began arriving from the depots at Stapleton (near Bristol), Normans Cross (near Peterborough), Mill Prison, Plymouth and from the hulks at Plymouth, Portsmouth and Chatham. Among them were approximately 2,200 who had served in the Royal Navy either as volunteers or 'pressed' men.* On the outbreak of war with the United States they 'declared themselves' as unwilling to take part in a conflict against their own country. They were immediately arrested and put into captivity, cursed at as rebels and traitors; some were flogged. Paradoxically a number of sailors at Dartmoor who had previously served in the Royal Navy received their back pay and in some cases their share of prize money.

* The R.N. was always short of crewmen due to expansion of the fleet during the war with France and to replace those killed and wounded in battle. The problem was partly solved by abducting likely looking young men in the seaports and stopping British merchant ships on the high seas and taking a number of crew members by force. American vessels were also intercepted for this purpose and although it was British crewmen that were sought there was no compunction about seizing American sailors too; this was one of the immediate causes of the War of 1812.

By the end of that year there were over 5,500 Americans on the moor. By this time they were well organised with an elected Committee in each prison block who adjudicated over disputes and generally kept order from a set of rules set up and approved by the men themselves. These are some of them:

'Regulations established by the Committee appointed by the Majority of Prisoners'

'Any person or persons who shall be found guilty of Treachery, Theft, or uncleanlyness, shall receive corporal punishment* - according to the Nature of the offence - and as the Jury Shall determine'.

* This meant a whipping with hammock cords.

'Any person or persons who shall be found guilty of makeing any neusance (except in the Necessary) shall be made to clean the same and pay one shilling.

'Any person who shall have cause of Complaint shall make the same Known to the Committee whose decision shall be definitive unless they shall see fit to call a jury'.

'It shall be the duty of the Committee - to appoint 8 men out of the Sd. Committee to attend in the Cook house, and 2 to attend outside and Inspect the provision'.

'Any one of the Committee who shall be guilty of a breach of any of the foregoing Articles, Shall pay double'.

Note: all spellings as per the original book of rules.

Soon they were organised in other ways – in escape attempts. The most determined and spectacular of these was a tunnel excavated from within one of the prison blocks with the intention of undermining the boundary walls to freedom. It was to be a mass breakout but somehow Captain Shortland's suspicions were aroused and after a search the tunnel was discovered and blocked up. A second tunnel was begun but again the plot was uncovered and the workings stopped up with stones. Those involved thought they had been betrayed when one of their number was suddenly whisked away by the guards, probably for his own safety.

Throughout their confinement American prisoners everywhere were often given a hard time by their captors, some of whom had either fought in the American War of Independence or had friends and relatives who had. The 1812 conflict is often referred to by Americans as the Second War of Independence because, after more than thirty six years, the citizens of that country were still regarded by many Britishers as rebellious rogues and traitors. Another motive for the often cruel and heartless treatment they got was to humiliate and weaken them to the point where they would volunteer for service in the Royal Navy as a way out of their predicament. To their credit very few took up this option and those who did were quickly taken out of the prisons to protect them from the wrath of their countrymen.

The notorious No. 4 block was again put to use as a segregated area just as the French had done, this time to isolate the negroes and mulattos from the whites. The 'Black Jacks' as they were called suffered the most from sickness and death (roughly one third of all Americans who died at Dartmoor were from this group). The white men alleged this was because they were unclean and accused them of stealing as another excuse to be rid of them. In fact they formed a very orderly society, held regular religious services and generally set an example in peaceful good behaviour. Social outcasts were also banished to No. 4 where they became known as the 'Rough Alleys'. Many of them were British sailors or deserters captured aboard American ships and were troublemakers of the worst kind. Altogether this group were despised by all and were the cause of much disruption by taunting the guards, throwing stones, disobeying orders etc.

Towards the end of the year 1814 the Americans were becoming unruly and rebellious. They hated the place. They hated the wet and the cold; hated the Militia guards; were disgusted with their treatment in general and the heavy-handed punishments awarded for what they regarded as minor infringements. They were incensed when some officers swaggered into the prison and boasted how the full might of British arms (including the victorious Peninsula army) had been sent to fight them on their own territory now the French war was over. With the situation worsening the 1st Somerset Regiment of Militia, reported to be 'distinguished for their Discipline and Good Conduct', arrived at the Depot in November to take up guard duty.

What the prisoners were about to suffer was a shocking tragedy before their release and joyful homecoming.

Reconciliation. The flags of Three Nations hang side by side inside Princetown Parish Church.

THE FINAL EPISODE

High hopes, tragedy and horror marked the last four months of the American's detention at Dartmoor Depot

The War of 1812 ended very appropriately on Christmas Eve 1814 when representatives of the two sides signed the Treaty of Ghent. The news reached Dartmoor Depot on 29th December and was received with jubilation by the Yankees. The Treaty had to be ratified by their government however and the Royal Navy sloop 'Favourite' was despatched to the United States for the precious document to be approved. The American public were equally joyful:

"New York, Saturday Evening, 9 o'clock, February 11, 1815.
PEACE.
"The great and joyful news of PEACE between the United States and Great Britain reached this city this evening by the British sloop of war *Favorite*, **the Hon. J. U. Mowatt, Esq., commander, in forty-two days from Plymouth.**

"Henry Carroll, Esq., Secretary of the American Legation at Ghent, is the welcome bearer of the treaty, which was signed at Ghent on the 24th December by the respective commissioners, and ratified by the British government on the 28th December. Mr. Baker, late Secretary to the British Legation at Washington, has also arrived in the sloop of war with a copy of the treaty ratified by the British government."

The ship arrived back in England on 14th March 1815 and the fighting, which had been suspended, finally and officially ceased.

Before this the prisoners had endured another outbreak of smallpox of a deadly nature which they called the 'African Pox'. It happened in the winter of 1814/1815 when more than 200 Americans died out of a total of 271 who are known to have perished on the moor. Dr. George MaGrath, the resident Royal Navy Surgeon, laboured day and night to try and save as many as he could by vaccination (a newly developed preventative at that time). There can be no doubt that but for his endeavours many more would have died. An investigation into the outbreak concluded the disease had spread mainly because of the impure air in the prison blocks. A test established a temperature of thirty eight degrees Farenheit outside one of the blocks when the temperature inside reached fifty six degrees Farenheit due to the 'windows' being blocked up to stifle the draught and the closely packed bodies of sleeping men. Orders were given to provide better ventilation and for the men to vacate their prisons during the day and air their bedding.

In February Captain Shortland, in an act of compassion and consideration now hostilities had ended, ordered the release of the occupants of the Black Hole for half an hour each day for the purpose of taking exercise and a breath of fresh air. One of them managed to escape into the prison yards where he was greeted with shouts of triumph and spirited away into hiding. A prolonged search lasting several days amid laughter and derision from the Yankees was unsuccessful and Shortland's temper was aroused. The tense relations between inmates and captors worsened further after this.

On 26th March Napoleon managed to evade the Royal Navy ships patrolling in the vicinity of Elba and returned to France where he was received with elation. Thousands of French soldiers deserted King Louis XVIII and rejoined Napoleon who assumed his former position as Emperor. At Dartmoor the Yankees backed 'Old Boney' but for the Militiamen it was bad news. They were committed to serve for the duration of hostilities and could foresee perhaps years of further service they'd not bargained for. In any case they were already unhappy men because the majority of Militia units were disbanded when the French war ended and they felt they deserved to go home too.

The Americans, who were technically prisoners no more, caused further aggravation by yelling insults and throwing stones at the sentries. Things got worse in the first week of April when they were issued with biscuit (emergency rations) instead of fresh bread. With the war over someone was trying to cut costs by using up surplus stores. There was outrage from the men and an ugly situation was narrowly avoided when, after a confrontation with armed guards with fixed bayonets, their rightful allowance was issued. They had threatened a mass breakout should their bread ration be withheld and in doing so created alarm and further mistrust between themselves and their guardians. On top of all this there was acute discontent because of delays in getting them repatriated (there was difficulty in finding cartel ships to take them) and as a consequence the Depot now seethed with suppressed anger and frustration. A spark was all that was required to cause an uncontrollable eruption and that spark was ignited on 6th April 1815.

On that memorable day there occurred an incident that brought death and terror to the inmates and dishonour to the Militia soldiers which was never absolved. It began innocently enough as the day drew to a close when at 6 p.m. the men were summoned to go to their prison blocks to be locked in for the night. Because it had been a fine sunny day there was some reluctance to do so and among the stragglers were some boys playing with a ball*.

There were several young boys in the Depot, most of them ship's boys with relatives among the crews. They were kept together to protect the youngsters, seven of whom were under twelve years of age and seventy five under sixteen.

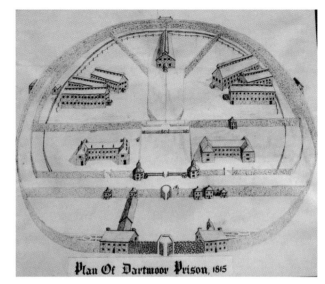

Dartmoor Depot 1815. There are now seven prison blocks - No. 4 at top centre of picture. (Courtesy of Dartmoor Prison Heritage Centre).

Plan Of Dartmoor Prison, 1815

As had already happened a number of times the ball was kicked or thrown over the dividing wall close to the Petty Officers' Prison and by chance at the very spot where there happened to be a hole. The occupants of this prison had been evicted and sent to live among the lower ranks to make way for soldiers from the barracks which was filled to capacity. The hole in the boundary wall was adjacent to the Armoury and was therefore under guard in case of an escape attempt. Each time the ball came over the wall the sentries tossed it back but at last their patience ran out and now they refused to do so. Angry Americans threatened to enlarge the hole and retrieve the ball themselves as a result of which Captain Shortland was immediately informed. He ordered the alarm bell to be rung. It proved to be a signal for disaster.

At the sound of the alarm hundreds of prisoners came running back out of the prisons and congregated at the entrance gate to the market square to see what was going on. Such was the excitement there was considerable pressure on those in front from the men behind when, either by force or the weight of numbers, the gate gave way and a crowd of men stumbled into the forbidden area which was the square. Just as they did so Captain Shortland entered the square from the other (main) entrance accompanied by two Guard Commanders and about a hundred soldiers. This antagonised the Yankees who were soon hooting defiance at the soldiers. The Agent found himself confronted by hundreds of men in a place they should not have been with the open gates an invitation for hundreds more to follow. The soldiers were ordered to form an extended line across the square to prevent the possibility of a mass escape.

The testimony afterwards given was to the effect that Shortland and Surgeon MaGrath both pleaded with the men to return to their quarters but the situation had now got completely out of control with the 'Rough Alleys' inciting their comrades to defy them. The soldiers were then ordered to the 'charge' position which meant they lowered their muskets and faced the crowd with bayonets fixed as the two sides approached one another.

There was evidence too that some scuffling took place and attempts made to snatch the muskets from the soldiers' hands. At the height of the free-for-all someone (it was never ascertained exactly who it was) shouted 'Fire!'

A volley of musket fire went over the Yankees' heads chiefly because the soldiers could not aim properly in the struggle that was taking place. All the same the fighting stopped and men ran for the safety of their prison blocks but the boldest among them saw there were no casualties and yelled 'blank cartridges!' A confused crowd paused and turned again just as another volley was fired into their midst – the soldiers patience had finally snapped and they were out of control. The sentries manning the walls creating a terrible cross fire as they joined in. Captain Shortland immediately realised things had gone too far and stood with arms raised in an effort to stop the carnage but it was of no use. Continuous and spasmodic shooting brought down dead and wounded men whilst the rest made a rush for the entrances to their prisons only to be pursued by soldiers who broke ranks, shooting and bayoneting without restraint. The proof of this was seen afterwards when an examination was made of the pock marked walls within the prison doors.

Someone shouted 'Fire'. (Painting by Paul Deacon)

Minutes later the firing stopped and the military left the scene. Altogether nine men were killed, six on the spot and three more died of wounds in the days that followed. Over thirty others were wounded.. Those killed were:

John Haywood, a black man from Virginia shot in the chest.

Thomas Jackson from New York (a boy of fourteen) shot in the belly.

John Washington from Maryland shot through the heart.

James Mann from Boston shot in the chest.

Joseph Toker Johnson from Connecticut shot in the chest.

William Laverage from New York shot in the chest.

James Campbell from New York shot in the eye (he died two days later).

John Roberts – wounded twice in the thigh (musket shots). Died 12th. April.

John Grey – wounded in the left arm (amputated). Died 26th. April.

Inquests were held on all these men. The verdict in each case was effectually the same i.e. *'Killed by the military in attempting to break prison'*.

'Another American prisoner also killed by the military'.

'Killed by the military firing to prevent the escape of prisoners'.

In fact they were no longer prisoners but free men waiting to go home. They were also unarmed.

The Princetown Massacre 6th April 1815. (Painting by Paul Deacon)

LAST DAYS

Americans never forgave the British for what happened in April 1815. At best it was an unfortunate misunderstanding but more likely a revenge attack by Militiamen goaded beyond endurance. There were two Inquiries into what the authorities called the 'Melancholy Occurrence' but which was more generally remembered as the 'Princetown Massacre'. Agent Shortland was exonerated of all blame. The evidence that was given by Americans and soldiers was contradictory and in the end nobody was held responsible or punished.

For the Yankees it was a heartbreaking event. Some of them visited the hospital and were appalled at what they saw. Amputated limbs were strewn around the operating tables and the groans of wounded men *'was enough to freeze the blood of the most hardened parricide'* as one man put it. All the dead had been killed by musket balls but several of the wounded suffered musket and bayonet wounds; some of them had been wounded five times –an indication of the fury with which the attacks were made.

To cap it all ships to transport them home suddenly became available and on 20th April the first Americans were released and marched out of the Depot for Plymouth and home. The first to be imprisoned were among the first to leave and as they tramped away a spontaneous cheer broke out which was returned by their comrades in the Depot over and over until they were out of earshot. It was July before the last of them left by which time the Battle of Waterloo (18th June 1815) had been fought and Napoleon was finally beaten. Approximately 4,000 French prisoners fresh from the battlefields came to Dartmoor later that month as the Americans were in the process of leaving. When in August their Emperor was sent into exile on the island of St. Helena they too went home and the Depot closed. In 1850 it opened again as a convict prison and has remained so to the present day.

The prison blocks you see now are relatively modern having been constructed with convict labour during the late 19th century. Several of the old prison blocks and the outside barracks were demolished to make way for them but a number of buildings from those far off times are still there including No. 4 block which held the Romans, the black Americans and the troublemakers; the Petty Officers Prison; the Hospital; and the Agent's House. All are in use today but for different purposes and after extensive internal modernisation. Externally they are more or less unchanged. Then there is the famed Archway exactly as it has always been with the inscription 'Parcere Subjectis' remarkably preserved.

At the rear of the prison and outside the boundary wall are two cemeteries, one French and the other American. The remains of those who died at Dartmoor were interred for a second time in 1866 when the original shallow graves became exposed by weathering and the actions of wild animals. They now lie beneath cairns surmounted by obelisks each bearing the inscription:

IN MEMORY OF THE AMERICAN/FRENCH PRISONERS OF WAR
WHO DIED BETWEEN THE YEARS 1809 & 1814 AND LIE BURIED HERE.
'DULCE ET DECORUM EST PRO PATRIA MORI'
('It is Dutiful and Honourable to Die for One's Country')

In 2003 the American cemetery underwent considerable renovation having deteriorated during the previous 133 years. Funds were raised in the U.S.A. by Mr. Burton Showers of Illinois, former Illinois Branch Secretary of the United States Society of the War of 1812 with various other societies and individuals lending their support. On 17th August a Dedication Ceremony was held in the presence of representatives of the United States Army, Navy and Air Force.

The Memorial before and after renovation.

Princetown's Church and the adjacent Parsonage were still under construction by French prisoners when their war ended in April 1814 and the Americans completed the task. The Parish Church of St. Michael and All Angels still stands, a proud monument to the men of America and those who served Napoleon. In 1908 the East wall and window required urgent repair and an appeal for help was published in the *New York Herald* suggesting this might take the form of a Memorial Window to those Americans who died at the Depot. The National Society of United States Daughters of 1812 (all members are direct descendants of those who fought in that war) responded magnificently with a beautiful stained glass Memorial Window paid for and installed by them It is a major feature of the church.

American Cemetery Memorials bearing the names of all the American prisoners who died at Dartmoor,

*The American Memorial Window in Princetown Parish
Church.*

The text at the base of the window reads:

*'To the Glory of God in Memory of the American Prisoners of War who
were detained in the Dartmoor War Prison between the years 1809 - 1815
and who helped to build this church, especially of the 218 men who died
here* on behalf of their country.*

Dulce Est Pro Patria Mori'.

* Now estimated to be 271. This latest figure was compiled by the late Mr Ira Dye
formerly of the University of Virginia, USA, and an authority on the War of 1812.

Another memorial of a more poignant kind can be seen at the entrance to
Prysten House which is at the rear of St. Andrews Church in the centre of
Plymouth. Mounted on the wall is the joint gravestone of Lt. William Henry Allen,
Commander of the United States Brig *Argus* and Midshipman Richard Delphey.
Both men died as a result of a sea battle with H.M.S. *Pelican* in the Irish Channel
on 14th August 1813. The *Argus* was taken as a prize and brought to Plymouth
when her crew were sent to Dartmoor Depot, the only United States Navy men
to go there (most of the Yankees were Privateers men). Lt. Allen, who had treated

British prisoners kindly on a previous occasion, was buried with full military honours before being laid to rest with Midshipman Delphey in a vault within the church.

Americans generally are very well informed about their country's history but very few who visit Plymouth are aware that their countrymen were once imprisoned at Dartmoor. They are surprised and interested when told and want to know more. Hopefully this little book will help satisfy that need.

Prysten House, Plymouth, showing Lt. Allen and Midshipman Delphey's headstone.

SIGNIFICANT DATES.

18th May 1803	Treaty of Amiens ends – Britain resumes war with France.
1805	Transport Office proposes Prisoner of War Depot in Devonshire.
1806	Work commences to build the new Depot.
24th May 1809	First French prisoners admitted to Dartmoor Depot.
3rd April 1813	First 250 American prisoners arrive from Plymouth hulk *Hector.*
22nd December 1813	Captain I. Cotgrave leaves and is replaced by Captain T. Shortland. Americans admitted to daily market to buy tobacco and soap.
February 1814	American Government allows prisoners 1½ pence per day. Black prisoners segregated to No. 4 block.
March 1814	American Government allows further 1 penny per day.
11th April 1814	Napoleon abdicates. French war ends.
20th June 1814	The French are being repatriated. Napoleon exiled to Elba. All American prisoners in Britain (except officers) transferred to Dartmoor.
24th December 1814	Treaty of Ghent. War of 1812 ends. H.M. ship *Favourite* is dispatched to America for the Treaty to be Ratified.
26th February 1815	Napoleon returns from Elba. War with France resumed.
13th March 1815	The *Favourite* arrives back from the United States with Ratification of the Treaty of Ghent.
4th April 1815	The 'Bread Riot'. Fresh bread issued after confrontation with guards.
6th April 1815	The 'Princetown Massacre'. Nine Americans shot and killed.
19th April 1815	First batch of American prisoners leave for home.
18th June	Battle of Waterloo. Napoleon defeated.
July 1815	Over 4,000 French prisoners arrive at Dartmoor from the battlefields.
24th July 1815	Last of the Americans leave for home.
August 1815	Napoleon exiled to St. Helena. Repatriation of French begins.
February 1816	All prisoners gone home. The Militia leave. The gates are locked.

For the next thirty four years the prison remained empty. In 1850 work commenced to convert some of the old prison blocks for detaining convict prisoners. Despite several threats of closure because of its remote location and expensive running costs, Dartmoor Prison has survived. Today it still plays an important part in Princetown's economy and the confinement of convicted men.

Her Majesty's Prison at Dartmoor.